DOUG FLUTIE

by D.J. Arneson

MODERN PUBLISHING
A Division of Unisystems, Inc.
New York, New York 10022

Printed in Canada

Book Number: 10310
ISBN Number: 0-87449-020-0

Cover Design: Marker II Studio
Cover Photos: Focus on Sports
Book Design: Linda Kosarin

CONTENTS

Chapter 1

"The Pass" 5

Chapter 2

Douglas Richard Flutie . . . 27

Chapter 3

Boston College 38

Chapter 4

On to Glory 49

Chapter 5

The Heisman Memorial Trophy . . 56

Chapter 6

The Generals' General 60

The "Flutie Pass" has become part of football history.
AP/Wide World Photos

Chapter 1

"THE PASS"

"If you went out for a hotdog, you missed two touchdowns."
—John Underwood, Sportswriter

The game football fans will remember for the rest of their lives won't be recalled because it decided a championship, since it didn't. It won't be remembered for breaking a record—though it did. Nor will it be recalled for being an exceptional game, but it certainly was that. The game is memorable because of one thing: "The Pass."

It happened in one play. The game in question was in the final seconds when—but we're getting ahead of the story. This is how it really was....

The Boston College Eagles' 1984 football season was just about over. It was Friday, November 30. The team was in Florida to play the Miami Hurricanes.

BC's record was 7 wins and 2 losses. The Eagles would finish the year in the winning column. The team was heavy with graduating seniors. For the players who were ending their college football careers, it was a season to be proud of. How proud would depend on the outcome of the last three games. Friday's game would decide one of them.

The Hurricanes were the Eagles' biggest foes. In football it's the big things that count, and the little things that make a difference. Playing on familiar territory in front of home-town fans is one of the little things. The game would be played on the Hurricanes' home turf: the famous Orange Bowl stadium. Chalk up one little thing for the Hurricanes.

The day wasn't what the players from New England expected from the land of sunshine. It was gloomy. They'd come from the north prepared to play under the sunny skies, and what they got was wind and rain.

But football is traditionally a fall sport. In New England fall means changing weather, and changing weather means wind and rain. Chalk up one little thing for the Eagles.

On the morning of the game both teams looked at the overcast sky with furrowed brows. The rain was driven by wind. They knew the combination could spell disaster. Any player who has ever tried to hold on to a wet football knows that. So could anyone who's tried to catch one. And anyone who's ever had to throw a slippery pigskin into the wind has more tales of fumbles, incompleted passes, and dropped balls than he'd like to remember.

It would be a passing game. The wind and weather would not take sides. It blows into all faces equally.

Nobody knew that better than the two opposing quarterbacks. Their calls would lead the teams to victory or defeat. Their arms would throw the ball or pass it off to a runner. They were the men on the field who would make the decisions.

Bernie Kosar was only a sophomore at Miami. His brilliance on the football field already had earned him an excellent reputation. In two years he'd passed for over 5,500 yards. That's over 3 miles! In a game that's fought by the foot, he was on his way into the record books. He still had two years left to play. When his college career was over, he was certain to be a top pro draft choice.

The Hurricanes' quarterback was a classic dropback passer. On a pass play, he would take the snap from center and quickly step back from the rough-and-tumble action at the line of scrimmage into the "pocket." Then he would search downfield for his receivers while his linemen beat back the charging grunts exploding from the opposing line to get him.

Towering over the crashing bodies that surrounded him, at 6-feet 5-inches tall, Kosar would unlimber his arm and wing the ball downfield where, most of the time, it landed in the outstretched arms of a teammate. He'd done it again and again in his two short years playing college football. The day in the rain against the Eagles would be one more time—but far from *just* one more time. It was destined to be special.

Bernie Kosar knew all about the Eagles' star quarterback. But until this day, they'd never met on the playing field. That alone would make the game special. Little did he know just how special it would be.

Doug Flutie knew all about his opponent, too. He'd heard plenty about the man he would face that fateful day when rival met rival in the rain. The Eagles' quarterback was a senior. He'd played college football two years longer than his foe. Flutie knew it was Kosar who was chasing his own passing record. Kosar had passed the football only 3 miles. Flutie had passed it 5 and a half! He was as ready for Kosar as he'd ever be.

But Flutie played a different kind of game. He was a scrambler, a quarterback who scurries around in his backfield looking for opportunities. Or making them when they don't happen

Running for short yardage, Flutie escapes being tackled. AP/Wide World Photos

Passing under pressure usually results in Flutie Magic!
AP/Wide World Photos

on their own. He could perform in the classic dropback style if he had to, but fans who'd watched Doug over the years knew better; he was a scrambler. Perhaps his height demanded it.

Doug Flutie was small for a college quarterback. At 5-feet 9 and three quarter inches he was certainly smaller than the man he would face. His critics were already doubting if he would be taken seriously by the pros.

Doug wasn't concerned about his height that day. His mind was focused on one thing: to beat Miami. He'd led his team to many victories in his career at Boston College. They had 5 this year alone. They'd suffered defeat, too. Although that was part of the sport, defeat was never in Flutie's game plan.

It's not likely that what happened that day was either. Although Doug was 40 games into one of the most outstanding passing careers in college football history, there was at least one immense surprise in store that nobody had planned.

Fans began to fill the famous stadium early. The sky stayed dismally gray. No matter. Football is football. Even the cracked and peeling paint of the Orange Bowl stadium went unnoticed by the diehards who were there to watch a clash of titans.

The two quarterbacks were the hot topic of

the day. Excited fans defended their favorite in the long minutes before the coin would be tossed to decide into whose face the wind would blow first. Flutie and Kosar were friends. They had met early that year, but on a different kind of turf. Like many friendly rivals, they had played golf together. Their scores for 9 holes— 44 strokes each, a tie.

Tension mounted. Until this November day, 115 years after the first college football game ever was played between Rutgers and Princeton in 1869, no two opposing quarterbacks had gained more than 300 yards each in a single game. This would be the passing duel of all time. The fans in the stands knew it. So did millions at home watching on television.

The bands left the field as the last stragglers found their places. Drizzling gray skies hung over the open stadium. The wind gusted miserably. Television cameras were aimed like electronic cannons, ready to shoot the action and beam it across the country. The rivalry and fame of the teams and their quarterbacks would not be limited to just Miami and Boston. National football history was going to be made.

The crowd roared as the ball flew into the sopping sky for the first of many times that day as the opening kickoff brought everyone to their feet. Many would stand for the rest of the game, afraid to miss the action.

Football fans flock to Doug for an autograph.

Flutie began to perform his special brand of magic at the first opportunity. He cocked his powerful right arm and hurled the gleaming ball like a missile to the waiting arms of his "Eagle-eyed" receivers.

Eleven times, the small, quick-witted scrambler pitched the ball into space. Eleven times it found his aiming point. The sure hands of Scott Gieselman, Kelvin Martin, Troy Stradford, and Gerard Phelan—especially Gerard

Doug and Gerard Phelan demonstrate just how easy the now famous 64-yard pass really was.
<u>*AP/Wide World Photos*</u>

Phelan—plucked Flutie's passes out of the sky and carried the ball forward for yardage and precious points. The scoreboard tallied an early lead for the Eagles, 14-0. The duel was only warming up.

Bernie Kosar was not going to be undone by his friend and rival from the north. The Hurricanes, too, had no intention of letting the visitors' romp go unanswered. They powered back onto the field with an answer to every one of Flutie's passes, a score for each of the Eagles' touchdowns. When the rally was over, Kosar and his Hurricanes had matched Flutie and the Eagles throw for throw and point for point. It was a 14-14 tie!

The dueling passing masters unlimbered throw after throw into the wind and rain. Ducks couldn't have landed with more precision than the falling footballs did through weather that could not dampen this contest of champions. The score climbed upward as the clock wound down. But the victor was a long way from being decided.

The fourth quarter opened. Only 15 minutes remained in the game. On the field the players slammed together like bighorn sheep, pounding out yard after yard. Passes continued to fly. Then the Hurricanes' hopes began to brighten. With only minutes left to play, they were holding on to a slim lead. The score was 38-35.

But Doug Flutie's day was far from over. Cool and calm under the rising pressure, he orchestrated an 82-yard downfield drive that ended with a touchdown. Now it was the Eagles' turn to sense victory. They led 41-38. It was a slim lead, but less than four minutes remained on the big clock. It wouldn't be over until it was over, as baseball great Yogi Berra once said, but it *would* be over...and soon.

The Hurricanes fielded the Eagles' kick after touchdown with the enthusiasm of a fresh team on the first kickoff of a game. They had possession of the ball, but less than 240 seconds to send the Eagles home losers.

The stadium thundered with the roar of delirious fans. "Can Bernie Kosar do it?" they wondered. "Can Kosar pull victory from the closing jaws of certain defeat?"

Kosar was under intense pressure as he came onto the field. Tense but unruffled, he huddled his players. They had four minutes and four plays to move the ball 80 yards.

The ball was on the Hurricanes' 20-yard line. The teams lined up. With their helmets nearly touching, the eyes of each lineman were fixed squarely on those of his opponent less than a hot breath away.

The Eagles' backfield danced loosely over the turf. They were ready to leap in any direction to pursue a runner or, more likely, to beat a

16

Hurricanes' receiver to another of Kosar's well-aimed passes.

Kosar snapped his head from side to side as he positioned himself behind his center, studying the Eagles' defense right up to the moment his hands closed around the ball. He called the play.

The 22 players were catapulted into instant action, each doing what they'd learned to do in hundreds of practice sessions and years of play. Lineman smashed head-long into lineman. Some Eagle defenders broke through the Hurricanes' line after Kosar. Others were stopped in their tracks. But somewhere in the confusion of controlled football chaos something went wrong. A penalty was called. The Hurricanes were set back 5 yards. They would have to try again. Now they had one less play, less time, and more yards to save themselves.

Kosar lined up his men one more time. The Eagles were ready. Then disaster struck again. Whether it was due to eagerness or nervousness, the play unraveled a second time and another penalty was called against the Hurricanes. It was hopeless now. The clock had ticked away a full minute and a half. Less than two and a half remained before the game would end.

It had been a splendid contest. Those who watched had not been disappointed. Those who played could not feel cheated. The duel between the quarterbacks had been more than anyone imagined. The elusive 300-yard-each game was ready for the record books—Flutie *and* Kosar would be in it. They had each broken the record in the same game! All that was left was to record the final score. And that, everyone was certain, was the one on the scoreboard as the seconds ticked away—Eagles 41, Hurricanes 38.

But Kosar wasn't finished yet. With his team on its own 10-yard line and only 2 downs left to get to the other end of the field 90 yards away, he called the fateful third play.

The ball was snapped. Kosar slipped back into the pocket, which was now behind his own goal. An Eagle tackler charged after him, his brawny arms grabbing for the tall Hurricanes' quarterback. Kosar's lack of speed was showing, but so was his quick wit and sense of balance. He eluded the tackler and shot the ball forward for a 20-yard gain. It wasn't enough for a first down. The Hurricanes' quarterback had only one more play to call to bail out his team. A fourth down kick was out of the question. There would be nothing to lose now to try anything.

Kosar went for it. The play earned a first down. The revived Hurricanes began a sweep down the field. They gained yard after yard as the clock ate up second after second. Incredibly, they scored. With 28 seconds remaining on the clock, the Hurricanes regained the lead. They were ahead, 45-41.

Everybody in the Orange Bowl stood as the Hurricanes' kicker lofted the ball to the Eagles. Across the country, television viewers who had reached to turn off their sets, sure the game was over, hesitated. They'd heard of the Flutie Magic. The Boston College quarterback had a reputation for doing the impossible. So they watched, not that anyone had a real choice. Everybody sensed something was going to happen.

Now it was Doug Flutie's time to demonstrate calm in the face of certain defeat. Surrounded by players who were all bigger than he, Flutie called a pass play, the only logical choice with only 28 seconds remaining to play. With surprising calm he threw. The pass gained 19 yards and another down for the Eagles, but it cost dearly on the impassive clock.

Flutie rifled another pass to the arms of his receiver. It was good for 13 yards, but more time was lost.

Doug was a long, long way from the goalposts at the other end of the field. They looked like a gate that had been slammed shut on the victory that only three and a half minutes earlier had been his.

Flutie called another pass play, but this one

With his powerful right arm,
Flutie hurls the football like a missile.
AP/Wide World Photos

ended in disaster. It was incomplete. Boston College was left stranded in mid-field, 48 yards from the goal line. The clock showed 6 seconds. In less time than it takes to sing one verse of "I Had A little Dog and Bingo Was His Name" the game would be over. Over, that is, unless the Flutie Magic could be turned into a Flutie Miracle.

The Eagles believed in miracles.

Doug Flutie huddled his team. In a hopeless predicament only the calmest heads prevail. Not the most sensible, but the calmest. BC had one play in their book that fit the situation. They called it "The Flood Tip." Others called it "The Hail Mary." Flutie needed a prayer. Maybe this was it.

The idea behind the Flood Tip is simple. It's the kind of play anyone who plays sandlot football understands. On the sandlot you'd call it the "everybody run as far and as fast as you can and try to catch the ball," play. It had an added attraction. If nobody could catch it cleanly, they were to "tip" it into the hands of somebody who could. The "flood" was the mad scramble of receivers who were supposed to rush downfield to overwhelm the defense.

Troy Stradford, Kelvin Martin, Steve Strachan and Gerard Phelan lined up for the last play of the game. Strachan, the fullback, was just behind and to the left of Flutie who stood over

21

center. The other three backs stood alone, far to the side of the facing linemen. At the snap from center all four would race to the far end of the field and, well, wait. It then would be up to Flutie, his right arm and his "magic."

The Hurricanes were also ready. Only three men faced the Eagles at the line of scrimmage. The rest were spread wide and deep. They knew the Eagles' only hope was to pass, even if it seemed hopeless to everyone on the field, in the stadium, and at home.

As the count for the play ticked down, tension gripped every player, challenger and foe alike. Flutie shouted the numbers from his position behind the center. His hands were sure and steady, ready to take the snap and go for glory.

Gerard Phelan was ready, too. He'd done a superb job all day. Ten of Flutie's well-aimed passes had stuck to his fingers that rainy day. One hundred seventy eight yards had been gained. One touchdown on the scoreboard was already his. He looked downfield. It was a long way to the cherished goal. But this time, well, he believed in Doug Flutie's magic, so why not?

Flutie took the snap and immediately stepped back into the pocket to set himself for the long toss. But disaster struck. Expecting a pass, only two Hurricanes' linemen rushed the small Eagle quarterback. One of them, Jerome

Brown bulled his way through the Eagles' line and took off after Flutie. The quarterback was as good as tackled if he stayed in the pocket.

But Flutie is a scrambler, remember? The chase is part of the excitement of football for the wee wizard. He tucked the ball and squirted out of the pocket to his right, sidestepping the plunging Brown. Now he was in the clear to do his thing.

Phelan had exploded downfield the instant the ball was snapped. He knew the way. He'd been there hundreds of times before. The problem was, who would be there to greet him?

The Hurricanes' backfield began to converge on their own goal line, the only place a pass this late in the game made sense. The Eagles' receivers were already on the way.

One Hurricanes' defensive back, Darrell Fullington, a freshman, saw Gerard Phelan coming. With Phelan covered, Flutie's favorite receiver would be out of action.

But Fullington let Phelan slip by. Perhaps he didn't realize Flutie could wing a wet ball that far. Phelan was on the Miami 10-yard line with nobody between him and the goal. All he needed was the ball.

Flutie didn't let him down. He had circled around the Hurricanes' Brown and was now at his own 37-yard line. He planted his feet in the damp turf. As the wind whistled through the bars of his mask and the sky continued to dribble, the wizard cocked his incredible arm and prepared to throw.

Doug Flutie's keen eyes saw his receivers racing emptyhanded toward the Hurricanes' goal. One of them, Gerard Phelan, his roommate and good friend, was the target he was after. The muscles in the fabled throwing arm tensed, making automatic micro adjustments for the range and wind the way a mortar is aimed on another kind of battlefield. There was no time left on the clock. It was now or never.

The muscles unsprung. Like a missile launched from an ancient catapult, the ball lofted high into the air, piercing the wind on a trajectory that riveted the attention of millions. The damp brown leather bomb went as high as it could, and then began to plummet to the ground.

Gerard Phelan saw it coming. So did the Hurricanes.

To reach Phelan who was in the clear, the ball had to skim over the fingertips of Fullington and Reggie Sutton, the other Hurricanes' defensive back on the scene of the miracle in the making. To reach it they would have to leap higher than the Eagles' hopes for victory.

The Hurricanes collided in midair. The ball shot through their arms like a greased pig from the sky. Now it was up to Phelan. but as luck

Doug prepares to launch the ball during a practice session before the start of the Tangerine Bowl Classic.
AP/Wide World Photos

would have it, his lightning sprint downfield was about to end in a tumble to the ground. And worse, not an Eagle was close enough to "tip" the ball up safely so it could be caught.

The ground was already rushing up at Phelan when the Flutie flip reached him. He closed his arms around the spent missile and crashed headlong to the turf. He was in the end zone. The Eagles had scored!

The scoreboard flashed the news, but a whole nation already knew what happened. Doug Flutie and his Boston College Eagles had tamed a Hurricane in one of the most memorable moments of football history, 47-45. It was the play of the century, the one fans would remember forevermore as "The Pass."

Chapter 2

DOUGLAS RICHARD FLUTIE

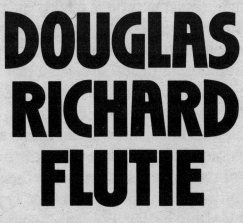

"Everybody is born small. If you want to stay that way is up to you."
—Anonymous

The names that blaze in Superstar heaven don't get there by accident. They don't get there by choice. It's true that ambition sometimes puts one person into orbit above the rest. With others, it's luck. Usually it's a combination. But one thing is for sure, nobody becomes a star without the most important ingredient of all—talent.

"The Pass" didn't rocket Doug Flutie into superstardom. He was already on his way. But how did he get there? What are the special things that make "the Flutie magic" possible?

What is the combination that makes this star super? A look into the life of football's newest legend tells the tale.

Natick, Massachusetts is a fairly quiet town. It's not too large, and sits a peaceful 20 miles west of Boston. It's just far enough away to have a character of its own.

Like every town and city in New England, Natick is governed by changing seasons. They say that staying one step ahead of the weather teaches New Englanders how to stay one step ahead of anything else nipping at their heels. Nobody has proved that better than the scrambler from Natick, Douglas Richard Flutie.

Doug's brothers are football fanatics. Here Darren (left), is shown in action during the Massachusetts Division I Super Bowl. AP/Wide World Photos.

There's another kind of season that changes in Natick, and all across America. It's the sport season. Whether you're a fan of baseball, hockey, football, basketball, or all of them, there's a special time of year for you and your sport.

Doug Flutie wasn't satisfied with just one sport. Like many young athletes, when the seasons changed sports, he did too. By the time he was ready to graduate from Natick High, he had succeeded in three of them, earning letters in baseball, basketball, and football.

But superstar success in athletics doesn't begin in high school. It begins somewhere in the life of a little kid with a dream and the courage to go after it. It also begins in a family that admires the ideals of sport and encourages them. Doug Flutie had the dream and he had the family.

Bill and Darren Flutie are Doug's brothers. Bill is the oldest. Darren is the youngest. Doug's the one in the middle.

Being a middle kid has some special advantages. You get to learn from the brother or sister who's older and you get to teach what you've learned to the one who's younger. That way you learn things from two sides. That's important in sports because to succeed you have to know how to accept coaching and you have to know how to work with your team.

The Flutie boys knew how to work together. Darren, who's 4 years younger than Doug, recalls how it was when Doug was about 9 and he was about 5. "He'd make me run with the ball, and he'd tackle me," he said in an interview.

The training must have worked because all three boys went on to play on the Natick High football team, and on their college teams as well.

Darren also revealed the deep interest they had in the game. Not just the playing, but the reasons behind the play. As kids the brothers would sit and watch games on television. "...and we'd wonder," he said. "If a quarterback would fade back and see nothing, he'd get hit or throw the ball away." It didn't make sense to the boys for a quarterback to get sacked if he could avoid it. "Why didn't he try to run, or do something?" they asked one another.

By the time Doug reached high school, his skills as a scrambler, a quarterback who doesn't stand still but "does something," were already polished. By college he would be an expert.

To be a star quarterback you have to know how to do more than just run with the ball. It's the quarterback who calls the plays. That takes the quick wit and cool mind of a strategist, someone who can figure out what to do before it becomes obvious.

Doug's father is Richard Flutie, a sports-minded integrated circuit analyst for an electronics company in the Boston area. Perhaps Doug inherited his quick, analytical mind from his father. Wherever it came from, two things make it obvious he's got one of the crispest minds in football. Doug's ability to call offensive plays is often unique. And so is his talent to spot an opponent's defensive move and to react against it on the run.

His father recognized Doug's keen mind when Doug was still a little boy. "Doug has always had the ability to design strategy," Mr. Flutie says. "He was making up plays when he was 8 years old. People thought that was cute."

Doug's mother, Joan Flutie, an athlete herself, also knew her son's mind. "He's always known exactly what he wants," she says.

Calling for the "Flood Tip" against Miami wasn't exactly what the opposition would call "cute." It could be called foolhardy, or genius, but never cute. But it was what Doug Flutie wanted. What it showed was a quick-witted, strategy-conscious mind at work.

Doug's young brother, Darren, might suggest that Doug's onfield strategy has another source. When they studied those football games on television as kids, the Flutie boys learned how the game really was played. Practicing on each other gave them the experience to try out their ideas. But it was something called "brainstorms" that produced the ideas. Calling for the Flood Tip was the result of a brainstorm, but it wasn't Doug's first.

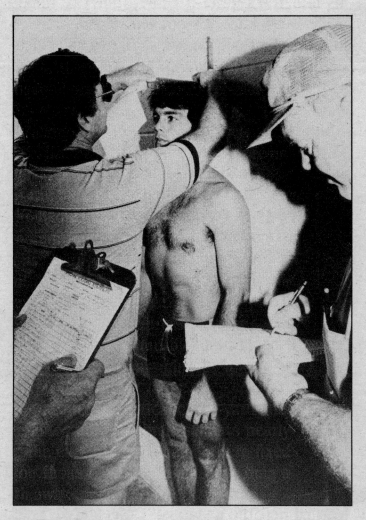

Doug's vital statistics are taken just before the 39th Hula Bowl game.
AP/Wide World Photos

"He's had a lot of strange ones," Darren says. "But mostly they're legitimate. It all goes by the book until a play gets messed up."

"Going by the book," is another reason Doug Flutie leads his teams so well. His father has something to say about that, too. "If you play by the rules, and Doug always did...it adds to his mystique."

By the time Doug reached high school his football skills were sharply honed. Bill, the oldest Flutie footballer had blazed the way for the others. When Bill graduated from Natick High in 1978, he gave up his quarterback slot to Doug. Bill went on to play football for Brown University as a starting wide receiver. He would graduate as an electrical engineer in 1983. But back at Natick High, it was up to Doug to carry on what was fast becoming a Flutie family tradition: football excellence.

Doug was a hustler, an athlete who played with the enthusiasm and spunk of a kid on a sandlot having a good time. It's a quality he still has. Like his quick mind, it's hard to say where such drive comes from, but it could be necessity.

Doug Flutie doesn't fit the image of the Hulk in a football suit. He's not a Master of the Universe in shoulder pads and helmet. Doug Flutie is a small man in a game of genetic giants.

Size, it's argued, is the key to a successful football career. Maybe so, but Doug Flutie is proof that's not always so. Standing straight, and full of steak and mashed potatoes, Doug Flutie is 5-feet 9¾ inches tall and weighs 173 pounds. If you don't give him the ¾", he complains, they say. But scoreboards from high school right up to the pros say he doesn't need the extra height.

Being small was never an issue while Doug was playing for Natick High. True, high school isn't college, and it sure isn't the pros. But high school players aren't exactly peanutsized. If you've got a big brother or know somebody who does, nobody has to tell you that. Doug played football, baseball, and basketball. That tells you something. He played so well, he earned letters in all three. That tells it all.

Doug played well at Natick, but he never thought of football as more than a game. He didn't consider football as a likely professional career. He wasn't even thinking of major college football. He didn't think he was very outstanding. "I guess I was a better than average quarterback," he said, referring to a game that was the high point of his high school playing days. But he didn't see a football future for himself.

The game was against a familiar Natick rival, Braintree (Massachusetts) High School. Maybe what happened was an example of what future football fans would get from this modest, "better than average quarterback."

Doug describes the game this way. "We had 30 seconds to play, trailing by a point, and I threw four straight passes to my brother (Darren) to go from our 19 to their 21. With three seconds left, with my brother holding the ball, I kicked a field goal and we won, 27-25—that field goal is what I remember most."

The play was a taste of other squeakers still to come.

Though Darren had a few more years to play for Natick, it was time for Doug to begin the search for a college.

While playing pro football was not in the mind of the quick, scrambling Natick star, college football was, even if it wasn't Division 1-A, the top division with the finest teams.

The search for athletic scholarships reaches its peak during the senior year in high school. Colleges with major sports programs often have their eyes on the cream of the crop of graduates long before the year is over. Things did not look good for Doug by the time he entered the final months of high school. Not one major college had offered him a scholarship. As good as he was, it looked as if he'd end up in a school with a small football program.

There had to be a reason, and there was. The college scouts were looking for big players. A college's prestige is often built on a successful sports program. A winning football team is important. The scouts who saw Doug mentioned his height. Until they did, "I didn't even think about it," Doug said. And then he added, "and, for a while, I started to believe them."

It was looking bleak for Doug Flutie. He'd go through a similar experience in four more years, but by then a whole lot of thinking about football would be changed.

But bleak was not black for someone like Flutie. At last a number of scholarships were offered. There were 5 of them, Holy Cross, the University of Massachusetts, the University of New Hampshire, Boston University and Boston College.

At first Boston College, BC as it is called, wasn't interested in the diminutive quarterback from Natick. They didn't want to take such a big risk when they could take a big body from somewhere else. Flutie was turned down for a scholarship. "My size was pretty much the reason," Doug says.

But the winds of Fate started to blow in Flutie's direction. The coach who had turned Doug down, Ed Chlebek, left BC after a 0-11 season in 1978. To replace him, the Eagles took on one of their former assistant coaches who had gone on to become the head coach at the University of Maine, Jack Bicknell. Bicknell arrived in the middle of BC's recruiting season.

Doug is an enthusiastic player as well as a fan, especially when he's cheering his alma mater. <u>AP/Wide World Photos</u>

The winds of Fate were also blowing favorably on BC as the next 4 years would show.

In his low-key manner, Doug describes what happened next in player recruiting at BC. "They were sort of scrounging around," he says. "And all of a sudden they were back in the picture. But I was the 33rd of 40 scholarship offers they made. It wasn't like it was a big deal. Really, I thought I might sit on the bench for four years."

Hardly. While it's true Doug Flutie was recruited by BC to play as a 4th stringer, nothing else that Doug, the coaches or BC thought then would ever be true again. Doug Flutie was on his way to making BC football history and then some.

Chapter 3

BOSTON COLLEGE

"I could see that this kid had something special."
—*Jack Bicknell, Head Coach, BC*

Doug Flutie was going to change the spirit of things around Boston College as it had never been changed before. It would happen almost like in a fairy tale.

Boston College, nicknamed "The Heights," is a thriving and lively college in Chestnut Hill, Massachusetts, a short bus or subway ride from Boston.

The school song is "For Boston" but it had been quite a while since students sang it because of an outstanding football season. The last time BC had been to a bowl game was the Sugar Bowl in 1942. The 0 win, 11 loss season the year before Flutie arrived may not fairly tell how things had been going, but it hints. On the other hand, student enthusiasm for their teams was always optimistic.

There wasn't a whole lot of optimism around in the fall of 1981. BC's upset over Texas A&M resulted in a 13-12 win, but it was hardly a victory. A decisive loss to North Carolina, 56-14, and another to West Virginia, 38-10, seemed to set the pattern for another disappointing year. By the middle of the season, BC's optimism was falling faster than the leaves on New England's autumn trees.

Flutie hadn't left the bench all season. His chances of playing quarterback were dim. In the final quarter of the game against BC's big rival, the Penn State Nittany Lions, the Eagles trailed 31-0. Doug toyed with the idea of asking Coach Bicknell if he could try out as a wide receiver. He didn't get the chance to ask.

Bicknell was facing the fourth loss of his first season as BC head coach. He scanned the bench. There was Doug Flutie, still in a clean uniform, untouched and untried. Bicknell made the decision that continues to have its effect on football to this day. He sent Flutie in, not as a wide receiver, but as quarterback.

"He went into that game, and it was like

Even under the pressure of an advancing Rutger's University defensive player, Doug sizes up the situation and passes off successfully. <u>AP/Wide World Photos</u>

someone threw a switch," Coach Bicknell says. It wouldn't be long and the whole football world would know Doug Flutie had something very special.

Doug wasn't that impressed. He put everything he had into the game, but what thrilled him was just being there. "I figured I could tell my kids that I played against Penn State in front of 80,000 people," he said about leaving the bench as a 4th stringer for the first and last time.

The game began to take on a new look. Something was happening to the BC Eagles, something they'd looked for and needed for years. If the team was the engine, Doug Flutie was the sparkplug. "This was great," he said, thinking back on that first chance to play college football. "The next thing you know, we're on a drive and we score. I was going nuts. We were all going nuts—"

BC lost the game, 38-7, but they wouldn't lose the spirit, ever again.

By the end of the following year BC's win-loss record had changed dramatically from the 0-11 the year before Doug Flutie joined the team. There were 12 wins now, only 5 losses, and a tie. It was a good enough record to get the Eagles to the Tangerine Bowl to play their first bowl game in 40 years. Although they lost to Auburn, 33-26, it was a sure sign that with Doug Flutie leading them, Boston College was back in the running with major college football.

How was Doug affected by all this? Not that much. He loved football, for sure. But by his own words, he didn't want to be a "big shot." He remained true to his earnest, honest way of life. He practiced hard. He studied. But his way of living, he says, "...is being home with a pizza and a cola and watching football on TV."

He continued to try figuring out the game with his brother Darren at his side in front of the family television set. With a tape recorder turned on to take Doug's "notes," the Flutie boys analyzed what they saw. "He'd explain every play," Darren says. "If it went wrong, he'd tell me why."

Attention to that kind of detail was turning a natural athlete into a superstar, but nobody knew it yet.

Doug also had his studies to attend to. For a time he was a computer science major. He had a strong background in math, so it seemed logical to study computers. He was especially good in calculus. It could be that's another reason for his excellent analytical skills on the football field. But he lost interest in computers and began to think of a career in broadcasting instead.

The thought of playing professional football was at least two years, if not lightyears, away.

Alumni Stadium is packed with fans as Doug Flutie leaves the field after another victorious game.
AP/Wide World Photos

Doug began to develop his particular style of play by experimenting during practice. The coach who recruited him for BC, Barry Gallup, says, "He knows there's no scoreboard. He sees how much he can get away with."

Scott Gieselman, a tight end, says about Doug's style, "In practice...it's almost like you're in the sandlot and he's saying, 'you run down to the tire and hang a left.'" He adds, "...you turn and look back and you never know

43

where he's going to be. A lot of times you just see the ball pop out of the offensive line. And usually, it's pretty much on the money."

Doug developed a special rapport with his teammates. He had to. His brainstorming skills continued right along with his maturing, textbook approach to playing the game. To keep up with him required players to sense what he had in mind. Gerard Phelan, Doug's college roommate and leading pass receiver said, "It's just being on the same frequency with him…it's a matter of trust…it's not in the playbook. It's a matter of understanding, I guess."

Guessing is something Doug did well, too. No play from the line of scrimmage goes exactly as planned. Once the ball is snapped, the quarterback is still in control as long as he can outguess the opposition. Flutie says he just loves to tuck the ball and take off, a sign of an instinctive runner. But when things break down, the scrambler and strategist acts on the run to figure out how to save the play.

Doug might flash a signal to a downfield receiver to go left as he dodges tacklers on his right. And if he has to, he'll make a pass that looks more like a basketball jump shot than a football pass. His job, after all, is to keep the ball and get the score. As long as he's in control, that's what he tries to do. "You have to make something happen," he says. Making something happen is what Doug Flutie does better than most.

Usually Doug's ideas and "brainstorms" made sense, but sometimes they didn't. More than once after watching films of the plays he's called that bear the unique Flutie style, he'd turned to Coach Bicknell to ask, "Did I actually do that?" Sometimes, it seems, his ability to make things happen surprises even him.

The student body at BC wasn't the only group taking note of the new look on their gridiron. Local fans in the Boston area, always on the lookout for a good game, began to show up for BC contests.

Ticket sales to home games began to soar. Twice in the 1983 season the Eagles played at Sullivan Stadium, the home of the professional New England Patriots. Forty thousand people watched each of those games. Sales for season tickets at the Eagles' own field, Alumni Stadium, the place a friend would later kid Doug about by calling it "the house that Flutie built," jumped 50 percent.

The "Flutie thing" started to show up on television. It was also in 1983 that the Eagles' game with Alabama was televised to the whole country. It brought fame to BC and their up-and-coming superstar. It also brought big bucks to the college. CBS paid over $600,000 to televise the game. Other telecasts brought in

$350,000 more. Flutie and the Eagles were more than a big draw, they were big money.

People across the country were getting their first look at the player who would be called, "the creative force in college football." Doug Flutie was bringing new interest to a national pastime. And he was becoming a star.

The danger in stardom is that it can ruin stars. Luckily, Doug Flutie wasn't impressed with himself. Even though he was becoming a celebrity on campus and off, he remained true to his own standards. He had his group of friends and that was enough. "Around the crowd I hang with, there's no extra attention," he says, modestly.

To that a BC professor who had Doug in a Communications course added, "This may seem funny, but he strikes me as a hero. We're looking for heroes. And in walks this young man who thinks that a great night out on the town is a pizza with his girlfriend." Now, that's a tribute because it says that Doug Flutie is a hero because he's himself.

In the meantime, the people who keep statistics were also keeping busy. After that fateful first game against Penn State when he passed for the first touchdown of his college career, the numbers started to pile up.

By the end of the 1982 season Flutie had gone to the air 348 times. One hundred sixty-

Flutie's Eagles teammates help him celebrate his 22nd birthday. AP/Wide World Photos

two of his passes hit their target. That's 46.6 per cent. The result was a total 2,749 yards and 15 TDs. In a game against Penn State, Doug set the nationwide record for the most passing yards in one game all year, 520 yards! The Eagles ended the year with 8 wins, 2 losses and 1 tie.

In two more years, a statistic nobody in football had ever achieved would come to Doug Flutie. It, too, would be in a game with the Nittany Lions of Penn State.

Fans and teammates carry Doug and BC head coach, Jack Bicknell, off the field following a BC victory. <u>*AP/Wide World Photos*</u>

Chapter 4

"Breathtakingly proficient, precision passing."
—Sports Illustrated Magazine

By Doug's senior year at Boston College the Eagles had soared higher than at any other time in their history. Under Jack Bicknell's coaching, the team's place in the school's history was assured. Certainly Doug's was. The student body was on a rollercoaster ride that seemed to go in one direction only: up. But it was Flutie's last year.

Bicknell was philosophical about what would happen when the season finally ended. "The place will be rocking when that time comes," he said. "I'm not sure (the fans) understand. This is not the football capital of the world. I'm not sure they know what they've been seeing. I may find a guy who throws it as well (as Doug), or runs it as well, but to get the total package? I don't know if I'll see that again. Maybe I will."

There was no question Doug's presence at BC was exceptional. His performance had been outstanding. Even he realized he'd done well. He allowed himself to think about the possibility of playing professional football. He'd already been considered for the prestigious Heisman Trophy, college football's highest honor. His chances for receiving it at the end of his senior year were excellent.

And there was the unbeaten record.

Nobody in the history of college football had gained 10,000 yards in career total offense. Like so many peak performance goals in sport, 10,000 yards seemed an elusive dream. Doug didn't know it when he tossed his first pass in that long ago game with Penn State that in four short seasons he would be within reach of the magic number. It would be in a game against the same team.

It was a chilly November day when the Lions and Eagles faced one another on the Lions' home gridiron, Beaver Stadium, in University Park Pennsylvania. Joe Paterson, the Lions' coach, said before the game that Doug Flutie was one of the most amazing players he'd ever seen. "He's unbelievable," he said. Paterson would know how amazing and unbelievable when the game was over. The Lions' coach would not be disappointed.

50

Until this game, the career mark for total offense was held by Jim McMahon of Brigham Young University. It was 9,723 yards.

Flutie still had four regular season games before his college career would be over. Barring disaster, he would break the record in one of them. The game with Penn State was the first.

The game started slowly. Over 85,000 fans had gathered to see the two rivals compete. The players felt the tension. By the second quarter only one score was on the board, 3 points for the Nittany Lions. The Eagles had nothing.

Then, on the fifth play of the second quarter, Ken Bell, an Eagle tailback, took a handoff from Flutie on a draw play that went perfectly. The back scampered down the field for 71 yards and a touchdown. The point after was good and the Eagles took the lead, 7-3. But it wasn't destined to last.

Soon after, the Lions' star quarterback, D.J. Dozier, ran for 41 yards to put Penn State in scoring position. Steve Smith carried the ball over for the first of the two TDs he'd score that day. Penn State would have to fight hard to hold their lead.

The Lions knew they had to keep the pressure on Flutie if they were to prevent the Eagles from scoring. The Lions' defensive unit didn't let up. Twice they forced Doug to fumble. They sacked him four times. And two of his passes were intercepted.

Doug closed out his college playing career after playing the 39th annual Hula Bowl.
AP/Wide World Photos

The score continued to climb, and so did Doug's assault on the career yardage goal. But it was slow going. By halftime, the Lions led by only 7 points, 17-10. Flutie was only three plays away from McMahon's 9,723 yard record.

He broke the record early in the third quarter. Gerard Phelan snagged a 20-yard Flutie aerial to put Doug into the record books. Doug had gained over 9,723 yards in four years. And there was still over a quarter and a half of the game to play, over 20 minutes to put together another 277 yards to reach the magic 10,000 yards.

By the final half of the fourth quarter the score was 30-23, with the Nittany Lions in the lead. There was time for the Eagles to come from behind when Doug Strang, in as the Lions' quarterback for John Schaffer who was injured in the first quarter, made two solid gains on third down plays. It put the ball on the Eagles' 39-yard line. Dozier then ran the ball into the end zone and the Lions lead increased to 37-23. The Eagles' chances were fading.

But Flutie regained his composure that had faltered in the earlier part of the contest. He huddled his team and called for a pass. A bare 4 minutes and 6 seconds remained on the clock.

Doug took the snap. He scanned the field for his receivers and spying Kelvin Martin, let the ball fly. It hung in the darkening sky for a moment as if suspended by the shouts of the thousands of fans who'd come to watch Doug Flutie do his thing. The fans weren't disappointed. Martin snagged the ball and crashed over the goal line for a touchdown. It was Doug's only touchdown pass of the day, but it closed the score to within 7 points, 30-37.

There just wasn't enough time to turn the trick. The Lions ran out the clock and the game ended.

But in the meantime, known only to those who sharpen pencils and jot statistics, Doug Flutie had surpassed the incredible career goal, 10,000 yards!

"I thought I played average," Doug said when the game was over and his name was in the record books. It was a typically modest statement from a player who takes his football more seriously than he takes himself.

There were still 85,600 enthusiastic football fans in the stadium when the gun went off. Although the night was growing cold and the lights had been turned on to hold back the darkness, they stayed to the very end as a tribute to Doug Flutie's "average" game, unwilling to admit he'd been beaten on the scoreboard.

Doug had passed for 447 yards against the Lions. He lost 26 yards running. The result was 421 net yards for the game and 10,003 yards for one of the outstanding college careers in football history.

Doug nervously
discusses his plans
to join the
New Jersey Generals
of the USFL.
AP/Wide World Photos

Chapter 5

THE HEISMAN MEMORIAL TROPHY

"Winning the Heisman would be the most important thing to him. It would mean he's fulfilled every dream he's ever had in football."
—Laurie Fortier, Doug's fiancèe

Winning the Heisman Trophy is college football's highest honor. The 25-pound bronze statue of a stiff arming ball carrier is awarded just once a year. The player who receives it joins a very small group of football greats. It's only been awarded 50 times. Like any award, the suspense over who will win it thickens until the very end.

Doug Flutie's outstanding college career was more than enough to put the BC senior in the running for the award in 1984. His ability on the field, his unique "brainstorming," and his overall excellence made him a major contender.

But he'd been there before. In 1983 he was edged out by Mike Rozier, the Nebraska halfback, and Brigham Young's fine quarterback, Steve Young. As the sports experts who vote on who is to receive the award gathered to cast their ballots in 1983, Doug said, "...I don't think I have a shot."

It was a little different a year later. By then Doug was a frontrunner. He felt the pressure when he said, "I can't help dreaming of the Heisman, but it scares me more than anything."

Doug's mom, Joan, had a dream, too. In fact, she had two. One was that Doug win the Heisman. The other was more personal. Mrs. Flutie had two sons playing football at BC that year. Darren had joined his older brother on the campus and on the gridiron. Mrs. Flutie's "last family dream" after the Heisman was to see Doug throw a touchdown pass to Darren.

It happened during the last regular game of the season. BC was playing against one of its biggest rivals, Holy Cross. Doug, a senior playing in his last regular college game, was the quarterback, of course. Darren, a freshman, was a wide receiver playing in his first college

The 1984 Heisman Memorial Trophy winner poses with his family and girlfriend, Laurie Fortier.
AP/Wide World Photos

season. Mr. and Mrs. Flutie were on the 20-yard line.

Eight minutes remained on the clock in the third quarter when Doug took the snap from center. He stepped into the pocket, cast his "Eagle" eyes on his scampering receivers and then, with his feet planted solidly, rifled a long, perfect pass to Darren who dashed into the end zone for a touchdown.

For good measure, in a play less than two minutes later, Doug handed off the ball to Darren who ran into the end zone for another score.

The Fluties had their dream.

On December 1, 1984, Doug had his.

At a grand gathering at the Downtown Athletic Club not far from Wall Street in New York City, the announcement was made that Douglas Richard Flutie was the 50th recipient of the annual Heisman Memorial Trophy.

Doug Flutie, considered too small to play college football had proved that there's no obstacle too high for someone who believes in himself. He was the best.

Chapter 6

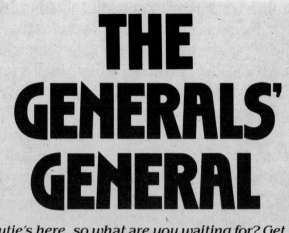

THE GENERALS' GENERAL

"Flutie's here, so what are you waiting for? Get your season tickets now."
—*New Jersey Generals radio commercial*

The Heisman was just the beginning. Doug's incredible career at BC was over, but at 22 years of age, his life was just starting.

There'd been a lot of talk about Doug playing professional football. Certainly he'd thought of it during the final years at BC when it began to look as if a pro career were possible. The trouble was, a lot of people said Flutie just wasn't big enough to stand up to the hulks that fill the pro ranks. Even Doug could get discouraged. "There's not a good chance that I'm going to play pro football," he said in 1983. "And I'm sure it would hurt if that day comes. But I'd certainly like to give it a shot."

Doug's hometown honored him with a parade when he returned after winning the Heisman Memorial Trophy. AP/Wide World Photos

By the time the Heisman was awarded, Doug's chances had increased, but he was still considered a long shot. Maybe he could play in the Canadian leagues, some suggested. Others thought the USFL rather than the NFL would be the place for him.

As for the folks at Natick, they knew the place for their hero was back home with them. As an honor, they named a street after Doug and his specialty, *Flutie Pass*, just to make sure that wherever he went, he'd still be with them.

There were other awards and ceremonies, even a handshake and a chat with another well-known football player who was now the President of the United States, Ronald Reagan.

But the big question remaining was, would Doug go to the pros? Would he even be asked?

The answer came in a bombshell announcement early in 1985. The USFL, a league only in its fourth season, would be Doug Flutie's new home. Donald Trump, the owner of the New

Doug and Mary Lou Retton—the medal winning Olympic gymnast—clown around with Bob Hope during the taping of Hope's Christmas special.
<u>AP/Wide World Photos</u>

Walt Michaels, the USFL coach and Donald Trump, owner of the New Jersey Generals pose with Doug as he displays his Generals' jersey.
AP/Wide World Photos

Jersey Generals, talked to reporters while speculation was still hot. "I don't know if we'll be lucky enough to sign him," Trump said. "But I'd go as much (money) as I think is reasonably ridiculous."

Trump offered 7 million, the most money ever offered to a football player. Doug accepted. He'd reached his dream. He was a pro.

And what is next for the incredible young football hero who said, "I'm not the greatest athlete in the world as far as height, speed, strength or anything else. But I'm a good blend of a number of things"? Probably a good blend of a number of things.

Doug plans to marry his girlfriend of over 5

Watching from the sidelines, Doug sizes up his opponents.
AP/Wide World Photos

years, Laurie Fortier, soon. He'll play football for the Generals, of course, and he's sure to be instrumental in helping the fledgling USFL hold on as a major influence in professional football.

Where else will football fans see the heavens blaze with the light of the brightest star to come along in years? For someone as talented and hardworking as modest, dedicated, Doug Flutie, the sky's the limit.